ADRIAN LEGG

Pickin' 'n' Squintin'

*Adrian gratefully acknowledges Flip Scipio for his help
in the preparation of this book*

Transcribed by Steve Gorenberg and Paul Pappas
All photos © Adrian Legg

ISBN 1-57560-255-5

Visit our website at www.cherrylane.com

And lo, it came to pass that a certain man, entertaining his fellows in the company of other minstrels in a lowly inn, did lose his purchase upon his flat-pick, which fell from his hand and did disappear through a crack in the floorboards whence no human might reach, where it mingled with a number of other flat-picks, much old and sour dried ale, and a coin from a neighbouring country.

He being a poor man, this was his only flat-pick, and there were yet several more numbers before the inn-keeper might pay them their hire.

So it was that he did perform with no flat-pick at all, but did exercise himself upon his many-stringed instrument with his naked flesh and nails, which did cause him grievous suffering and blisters, but which caused such a fullness of sound that he cared him not for his suffering and pain and from thenceforth did not encumber him with any other flat-pick thereafter.

And the leader of the troupe did say unto him, "Yea, verily, thou hast indeed seen wisdom and much increased thy sound. Play thou now 'The Soldier's Song' in B-flat ere we settle our account with our master and return again to our homes."

From the *Irish Sea Scrolls*, believed to be circa 50 A.D., from a sunken *Dun Laoghaire* to Holyhead ferry.

Notes

All the transcriptions here are the basic bones of the pieces. I play them slightly differently as time goes by, and you will find the same kinds of differences between the transcriptions and the recordings as between the recordings and live performances. I've tried to order them in roughly ascending degree of difficulty.

I now play "Kinvarra's Child" using a fifth fret capo, because I like the tonality at that pitch a lot and I think it suits the piece very well. There are other pieces in this book that I now play with a capo for the sake of the tonal change and the flow of a concert or album, but they are shown here in their original form as uncapoed pieces. I tried out a first position G version of "Kinvarra's Child" on a few players who read and contribute to the Usenet newsgroup rec.music.makers.guitar.acoustic. Most who kindly responded to my query described this as an advanced beginner's piece, so I believe it is an ideal place to make a point about tablature.

It uses simple open chord shapes that you will recognise, but the tablature shows the actual fret numbers with a fifth-fret capo rather than the conceptual ones that would apply if the capoed fret were shown as zero. The publisher's normal practice is to show the capo as zero, and number from it the same as if the piece were played in first position. Their purpose is to offer neophytes an easier grasp of the fundamental shapes. My belief is that ultimately an awareness of the actual fret numbers is more helpful and that to number otherwise confuses note and position recognition later on. So what you may recognise, for example, as a simple open G shape is in fact sounding a C chord when capoed at the fifth fret, and the tab numbers reflect those actual notes' fret positions. The publishers have graciously allowed me my own way here, so if it bothers you, you may abuse me rather than them.

If you get hopelessly stuck with anything and don't have a teacher or knowledgeable friend to help you, go to www.adrianlegg.com. If there isn't already an answer there, e-mail the management address with your specific technical query. It will be passed to me, wherever I am, and I will try to unstick you as soon as I have a moment. If your problem seems likely to happen to anyone else, it will be posted there with an answer, but without your name.

— **Adrian Legg**

Contents

The above titles can be found on the following CD's:
Guitar for Mortals (Relativity Records 1078)
Guitars and Other Cathedrals (Relativity Records 1045)
High Strung Tall Tales (Relativity Records 1224)
Mrs. Crowe's Blue Waltz (Relativity Records 1162)
Waiting for a Dancer (Red House Records 99)

LAST TRACK

Recorded on Mrs. Crowe's Blue Waltz

Music by Adrian Legg

Tune down 1/2 step:

⑥=E♭ ③=G♭
⑤=A♭ ②=B♭
④=D♭ ①=E♭

Moderately ♩ = 118

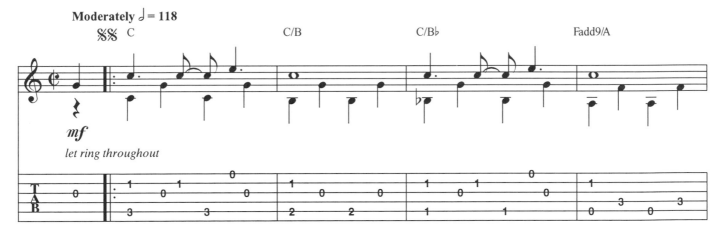

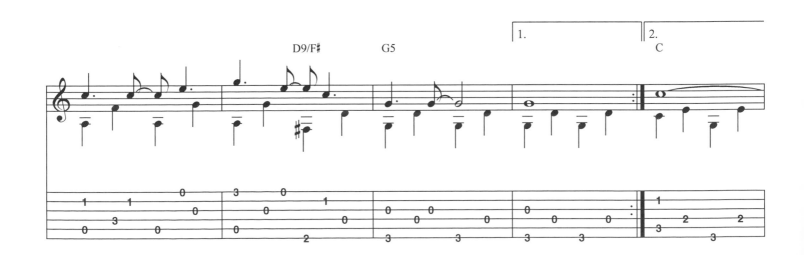

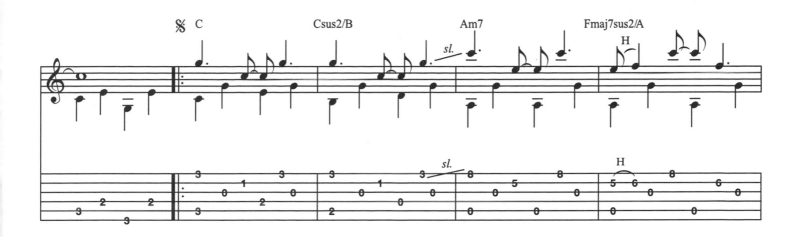

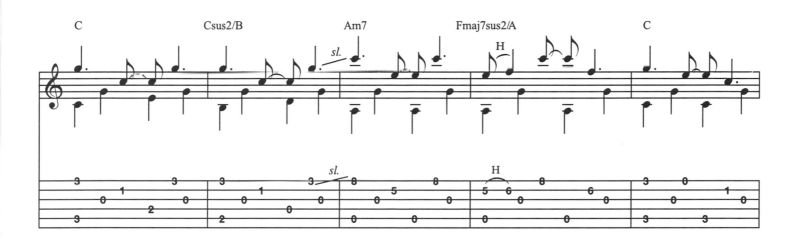

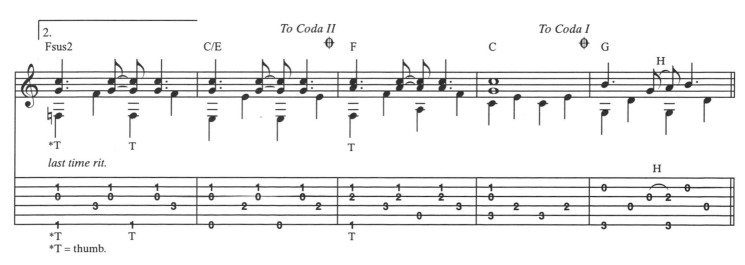

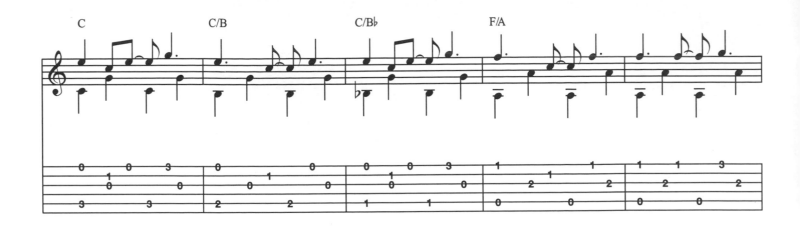

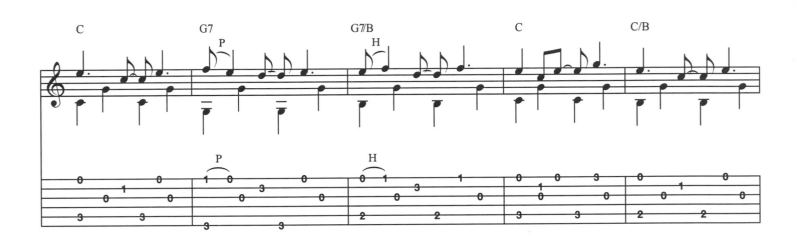

D.S.(w/repeat) al Coda I

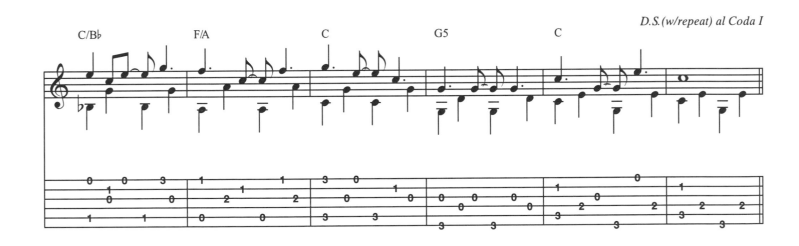

D.S.S.(w/repeats) al Coda II

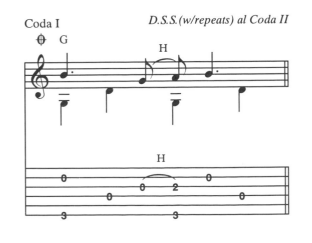

QUEENIE'S WALTZ
Recorded live on High Strung Tall Tales

Music by Adrian Legg

Tuning:
⑥=C ③=G
⑤=G ②=A
④=D ①=D

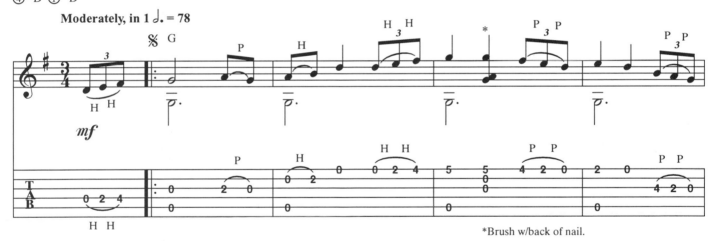

*Brush w/back of nail.

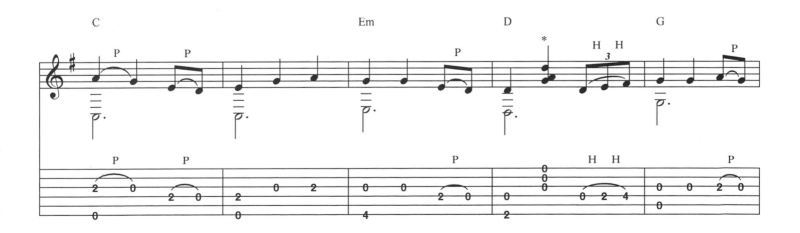

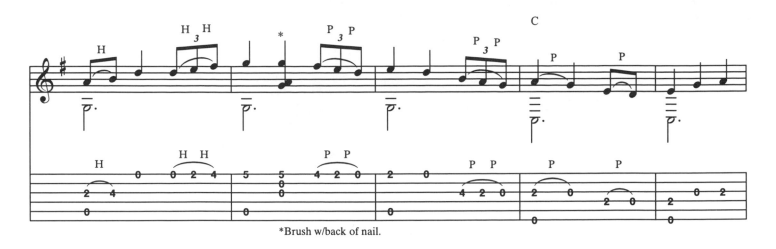

*Brush w/back of nail.

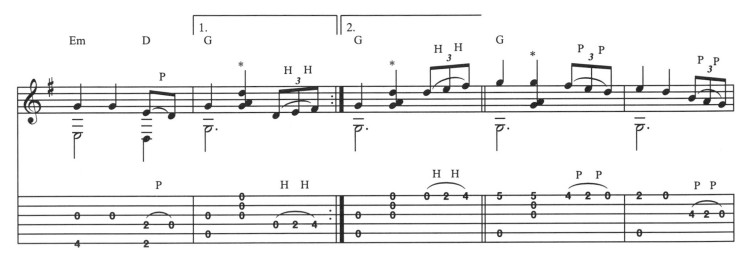

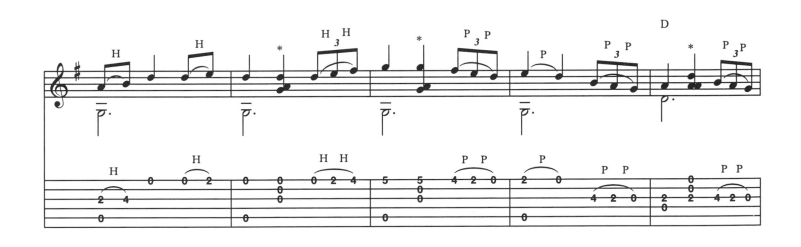

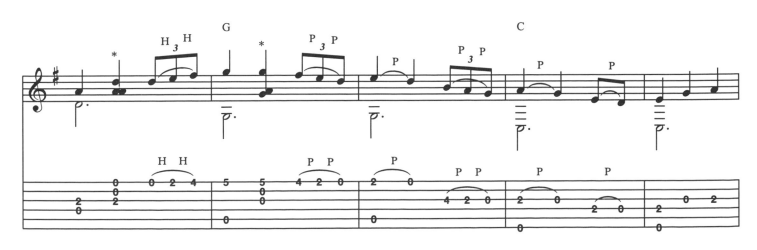

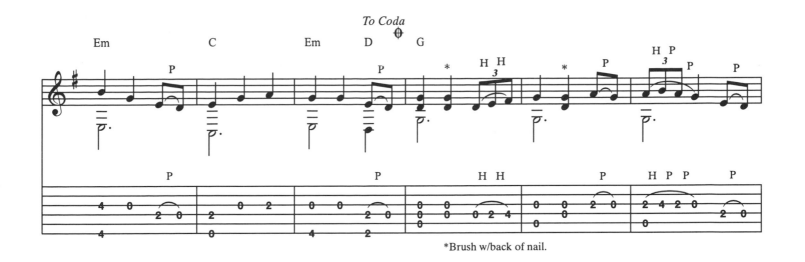

*Brush w/back of nail.

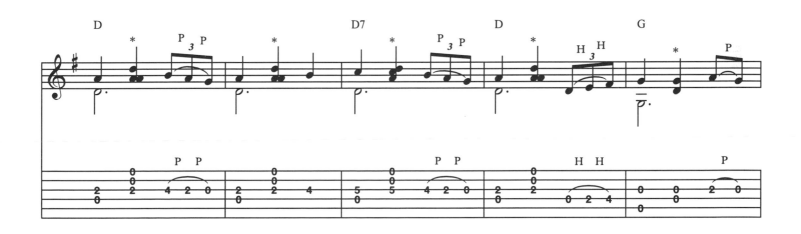

*Brush w/back of nail.

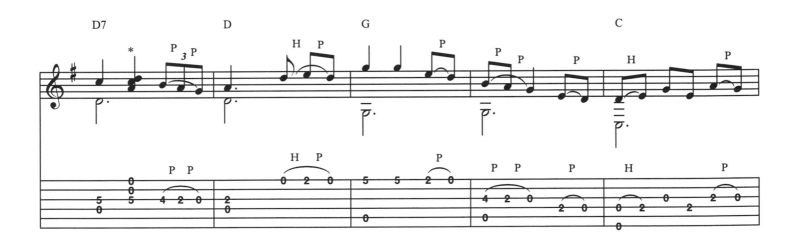

D.S. (take 2nd ending) al Coda

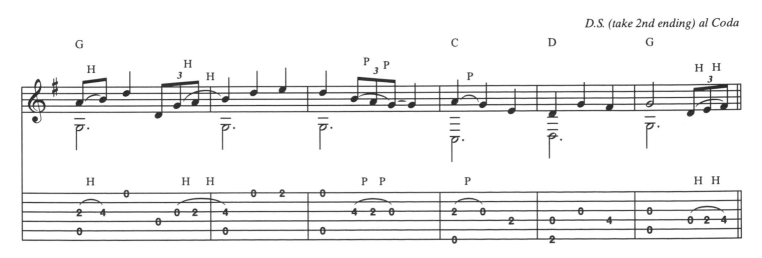

*Brush w/back of nail.

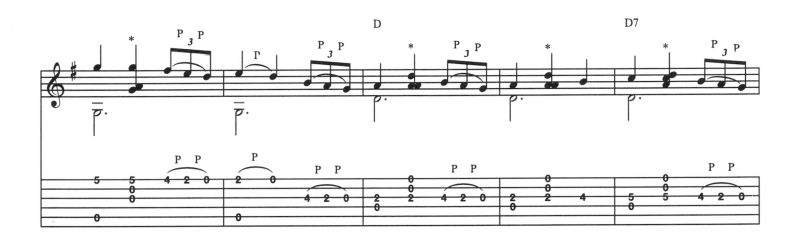

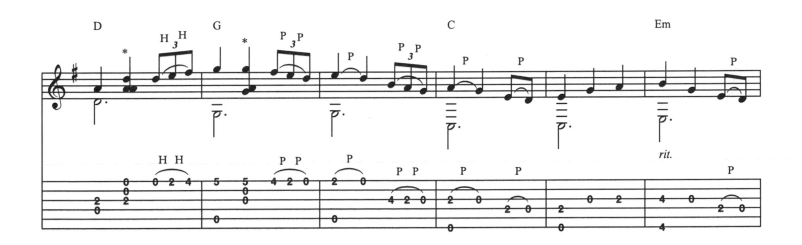

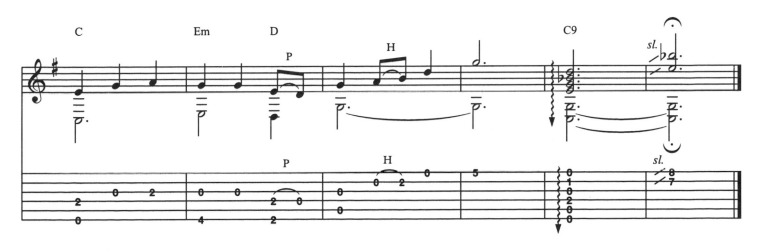

NAIL TALK

Recorded on Guitars and Other Cathedrals

Music by Adrian Legg

Drop D tuning:
⑥=D

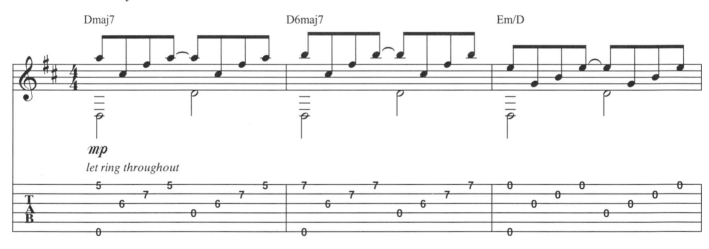

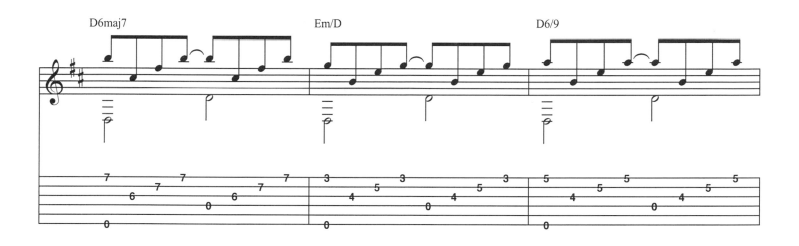

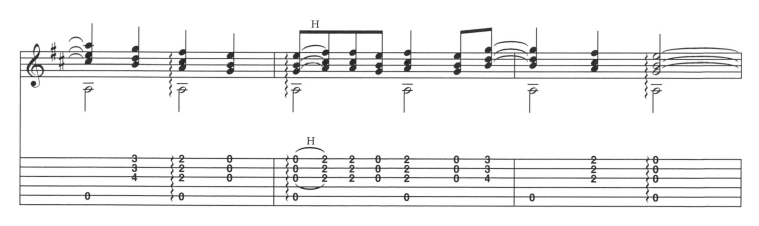

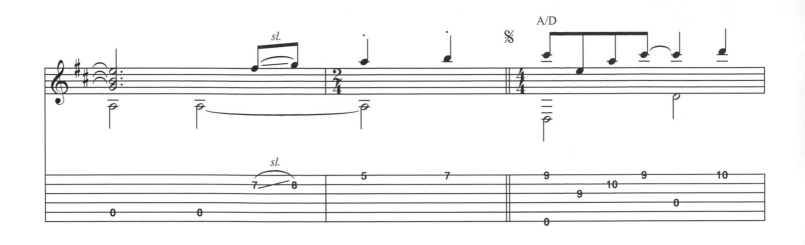

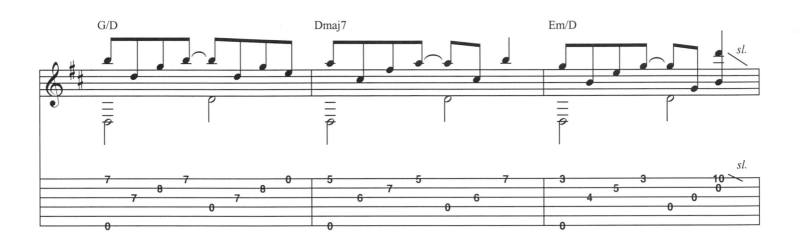

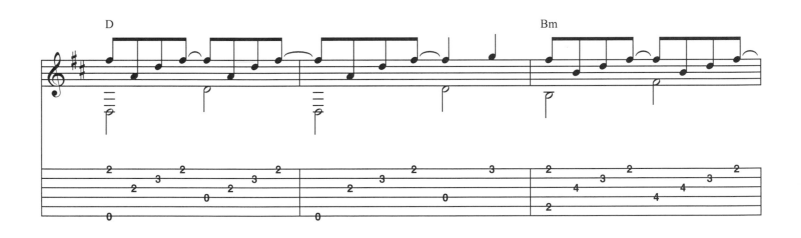

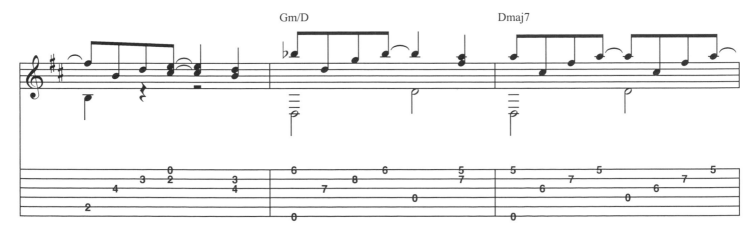

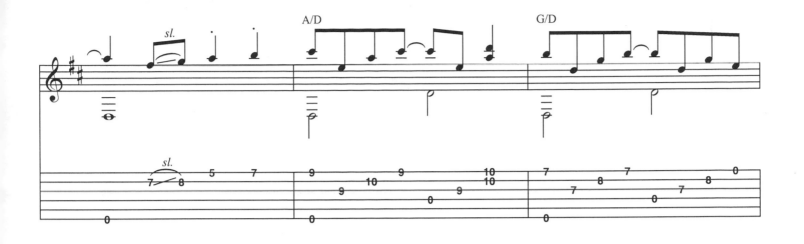

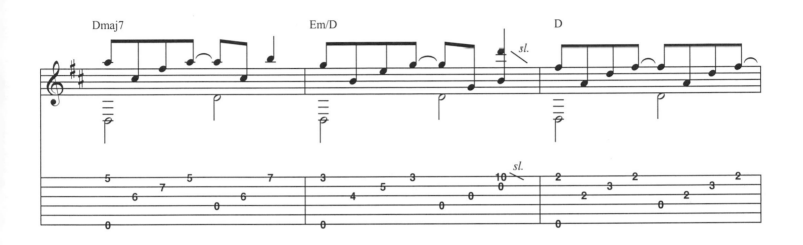

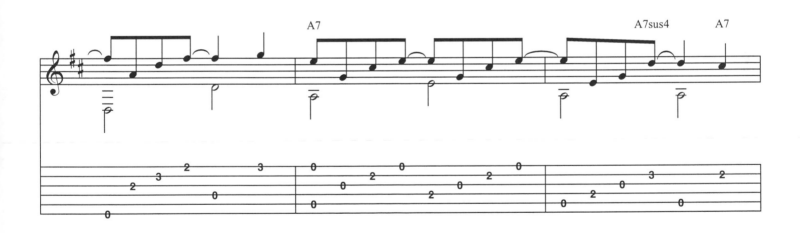

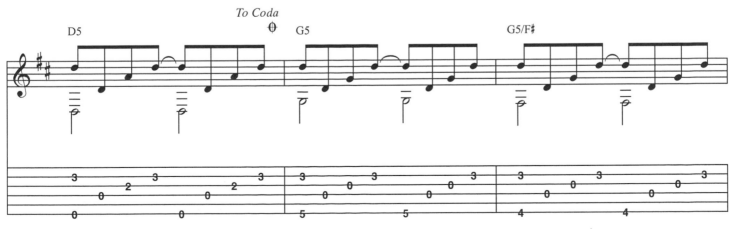

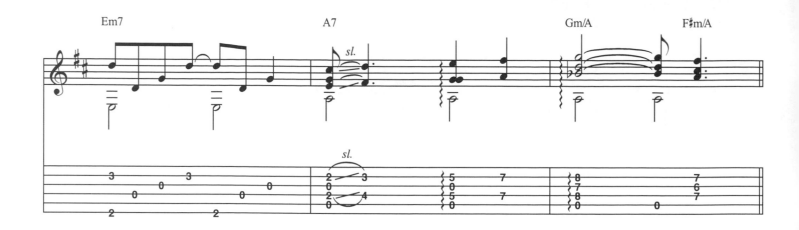

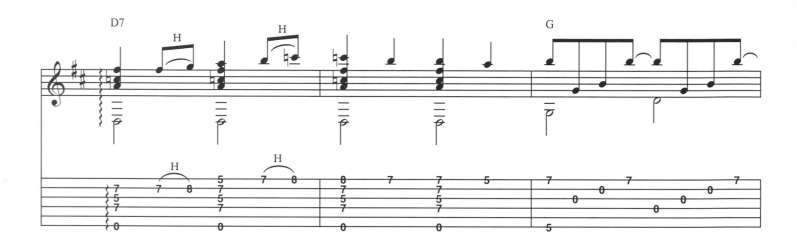

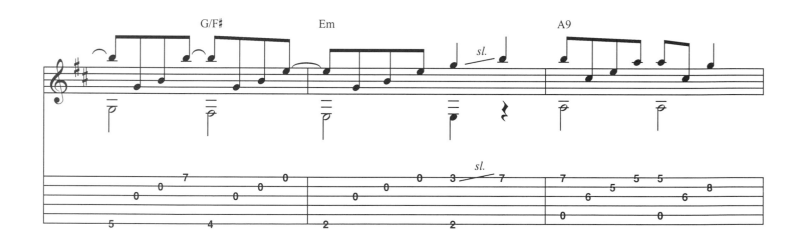

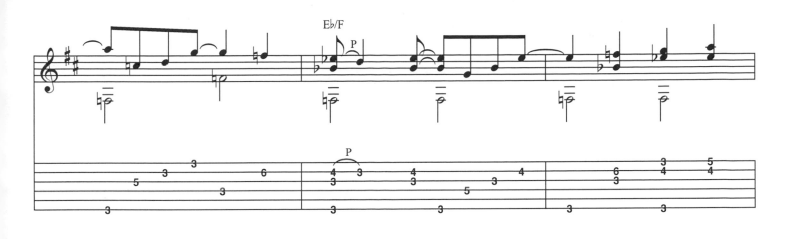

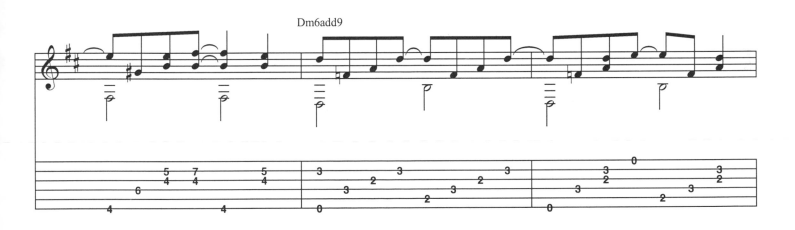

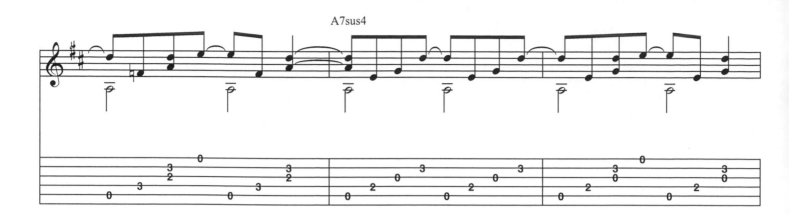

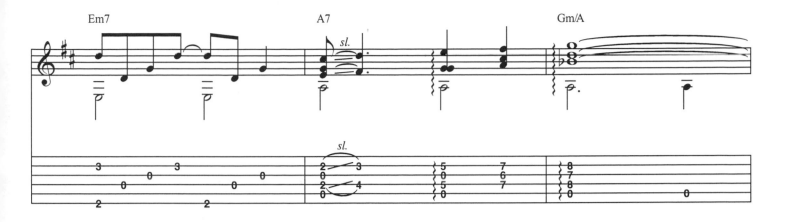

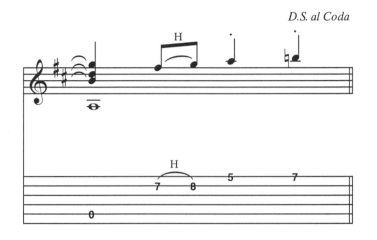

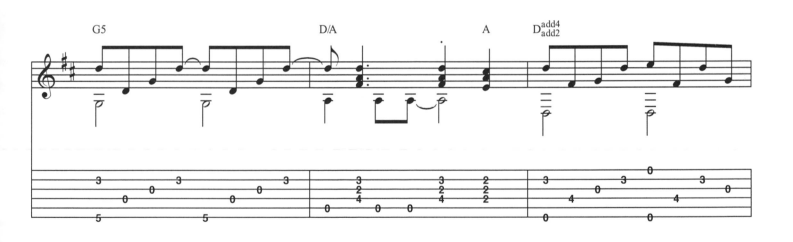

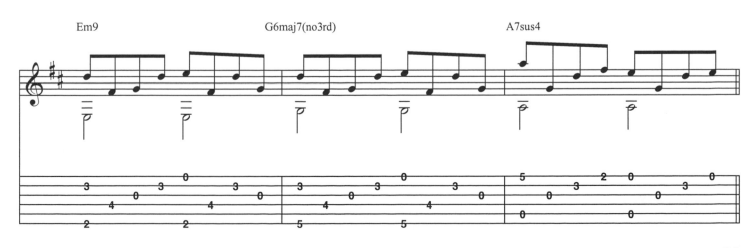

ANU

Recorded on Guitar for Mortals

Music by Adrian Legg

Drop D tuning:
⑥=D

Moderately slow, in 2 ♩ = 80

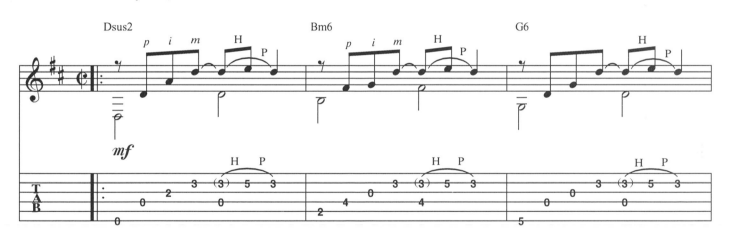

Omit 4th time

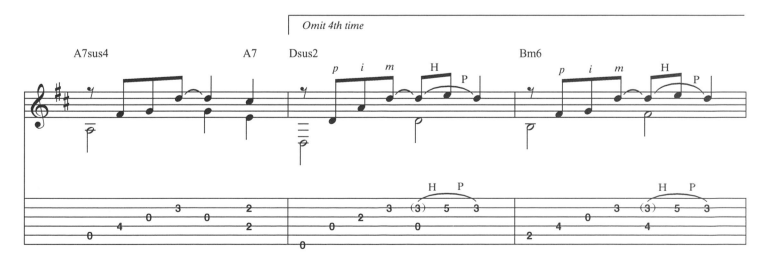

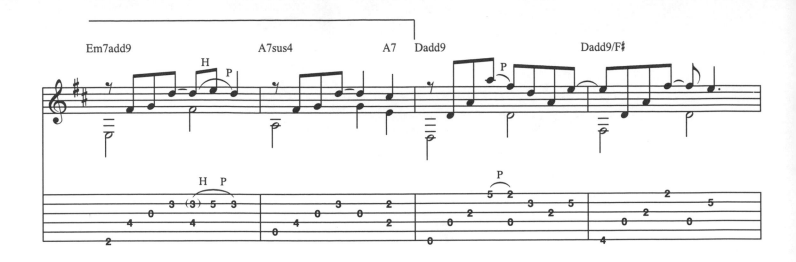

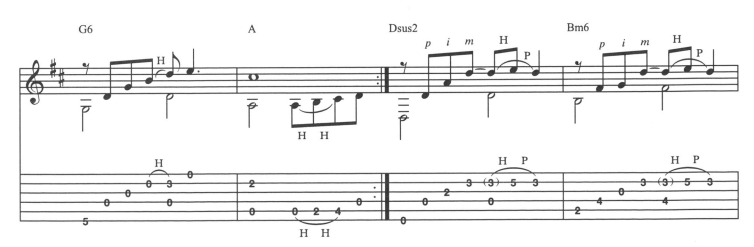

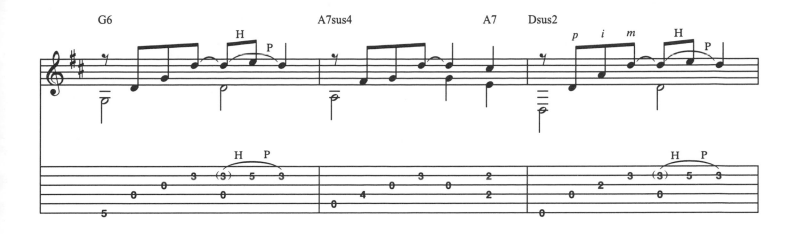

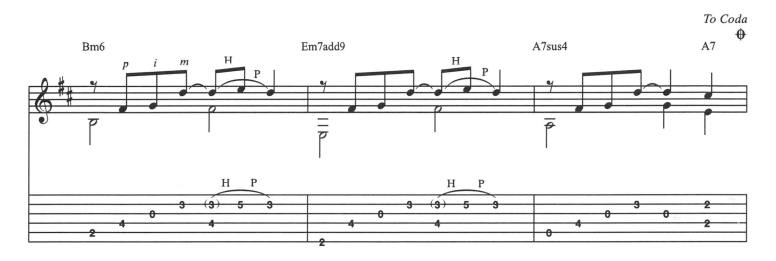

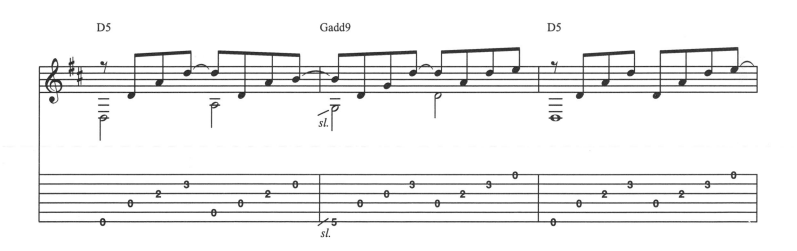

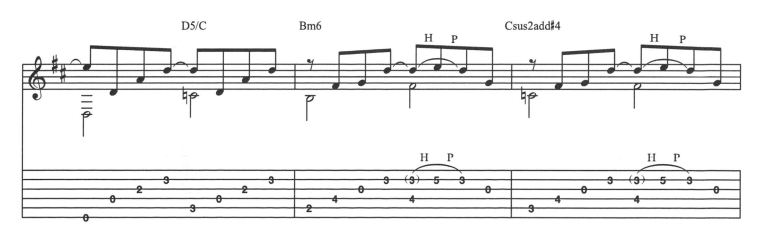

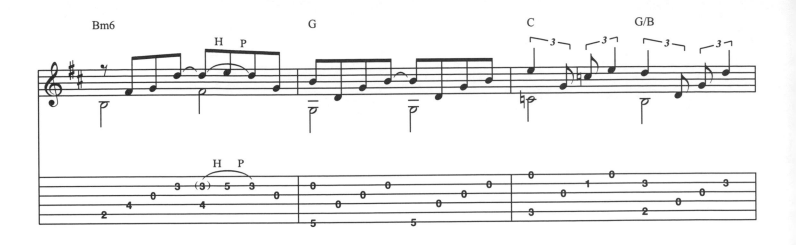

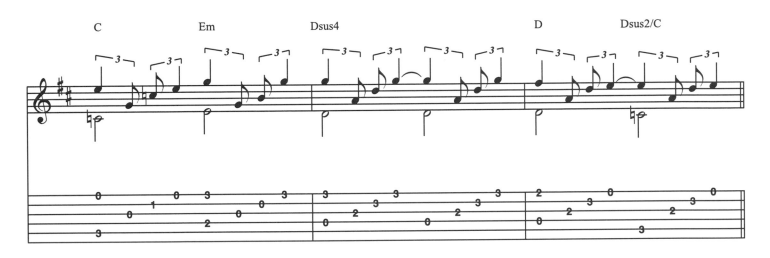

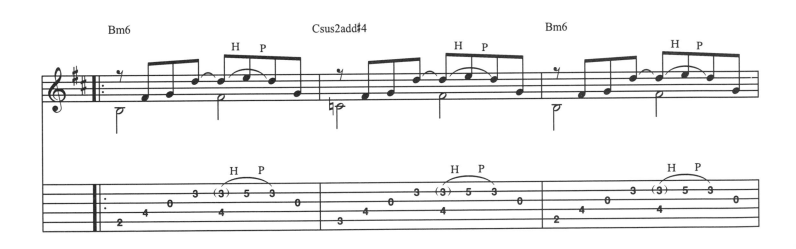

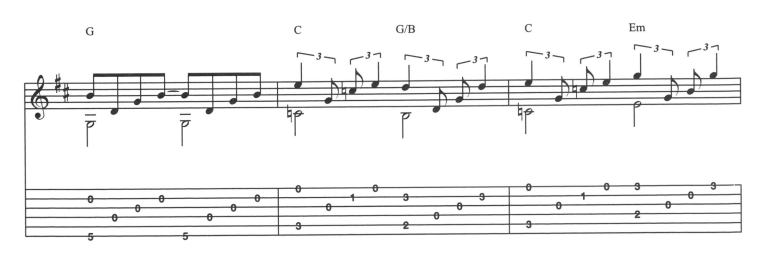

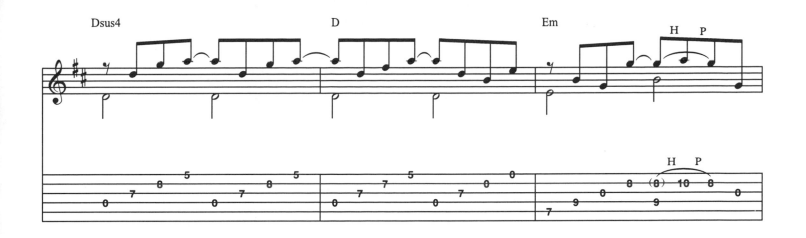

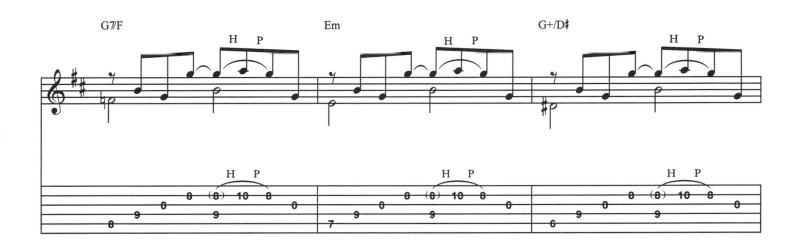

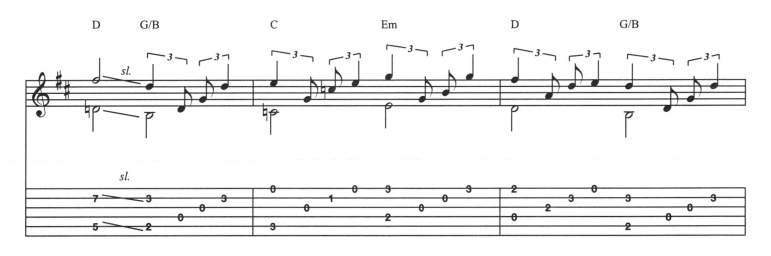

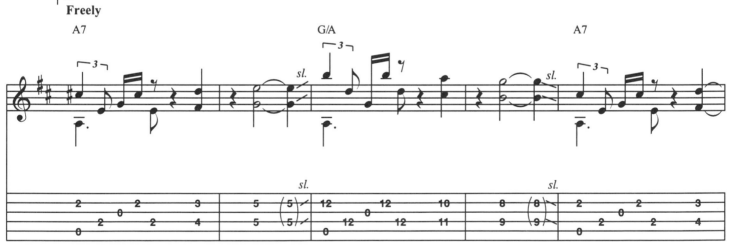

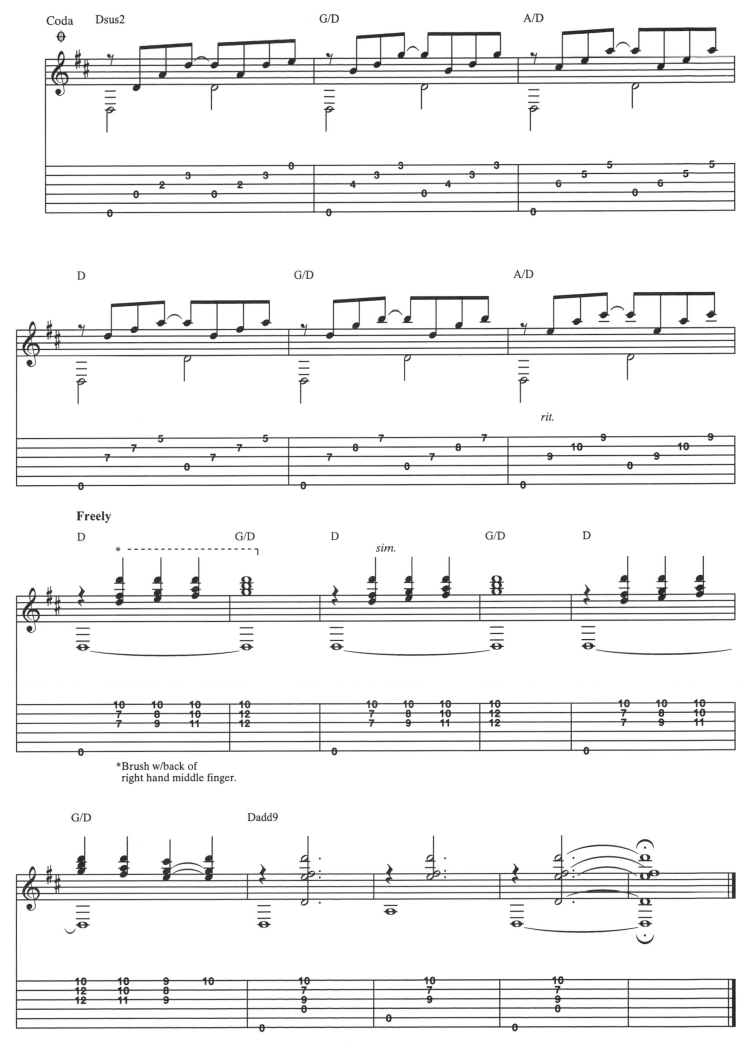

*Brush w/back of
  right hand middle finger.

KINVARRA'S CHILD
Recorded on Mrs. Crowe's Blue Waltz

Music by Adrian Legg

*Capo V

Moderately fast, in 2 ♩ = 120
Freely

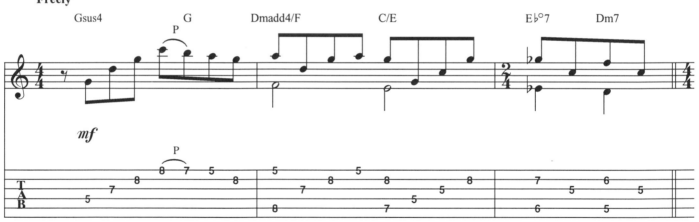

*Music sounds as written. TAB numbers are indicated relative
to nut. Open strings are "5" in TAB.

In time

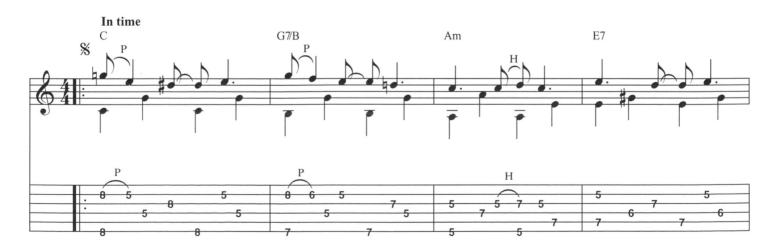

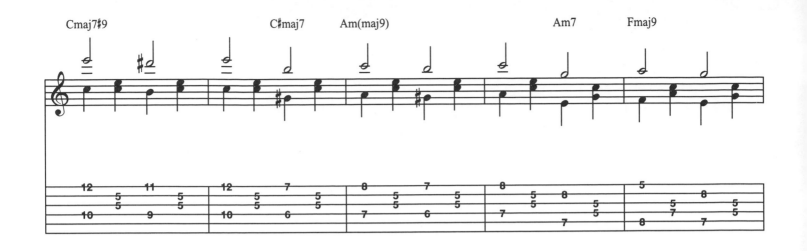

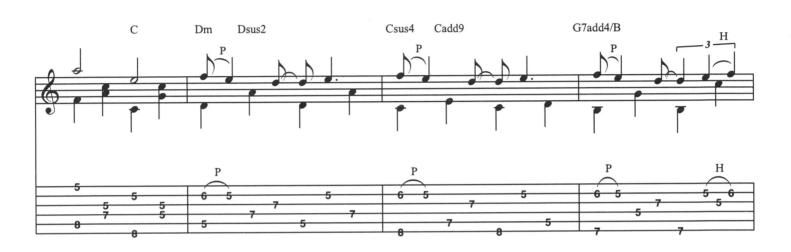

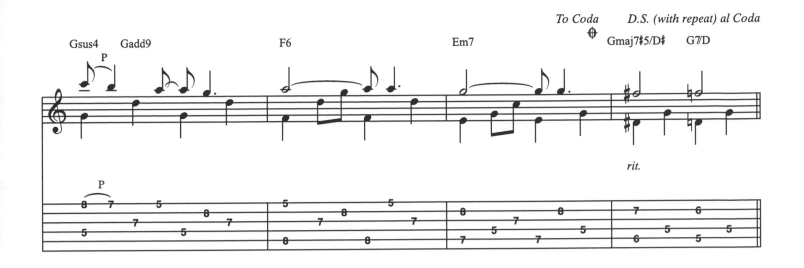

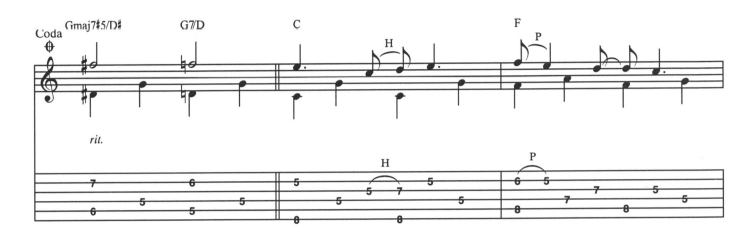

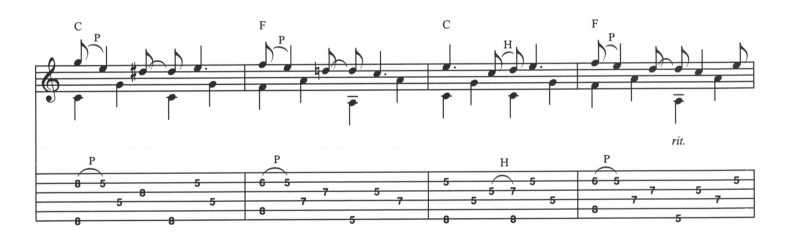

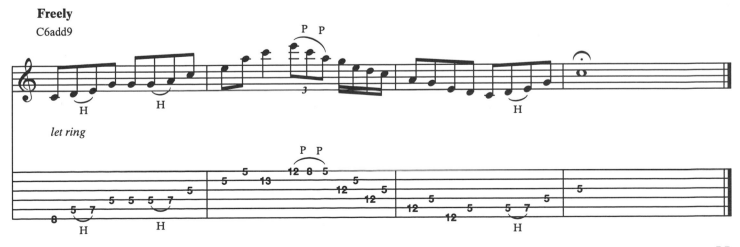

COGING'S GLORY
Recorded on Guitar for Mortals

Music by Adrian Legg

Tuning:
⑥=D ③=G
⑤=A ②=A
④=D ①=D

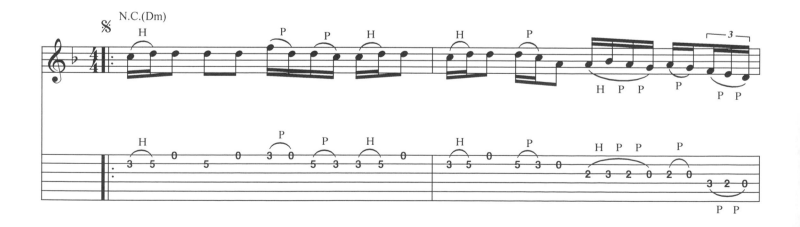

*Hammer on 2nd time.

*Hammer on 1st time only.

N.C.(Dm)

1.

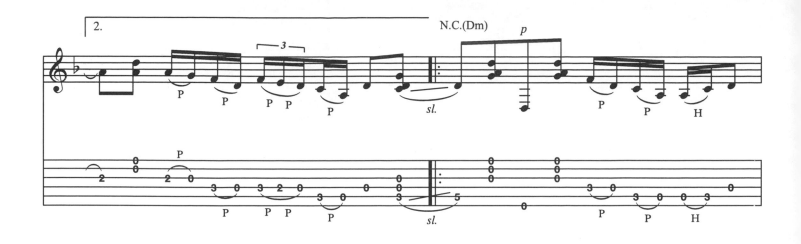

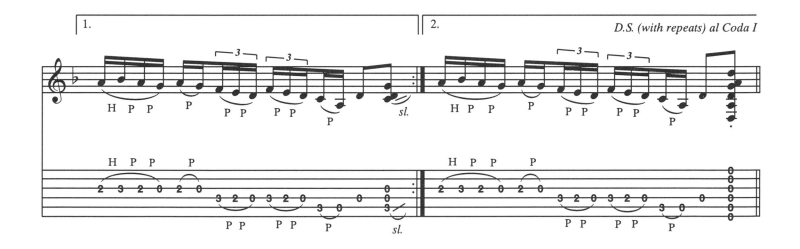

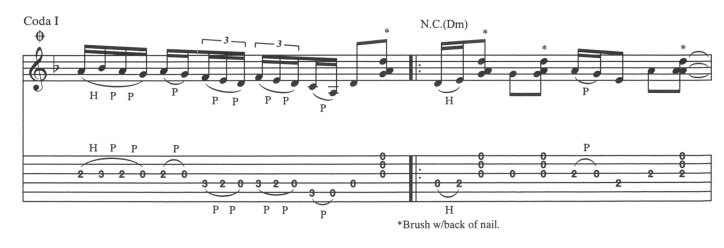

*Brush w/back of nail.

*Detune 3rd string
½ step w/tuning peg.

THE IRISH GIRL

Recorded on Guitars and Other Cathedrals

Music by Adrian Legg

Tuning:
⑥=D ③=F♯
⑤=A ②=A
④=D ①=D

Moderately ♩ = 120

*Brush w/back of nail.

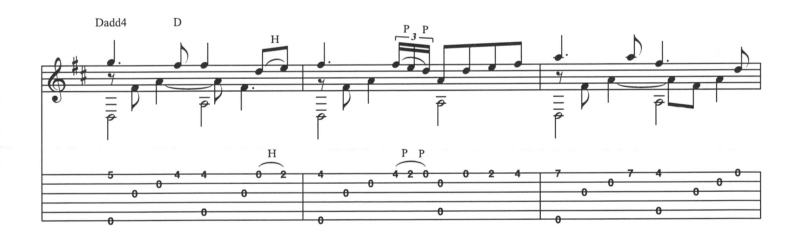

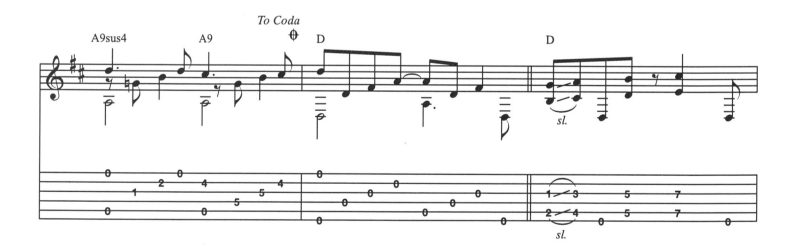

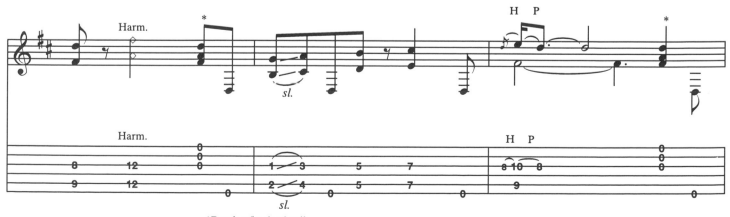

*Brush w/back of nail.

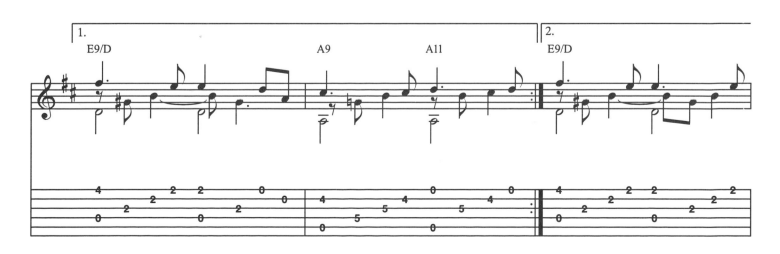

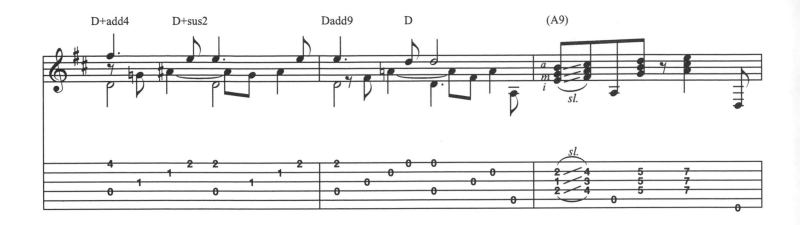

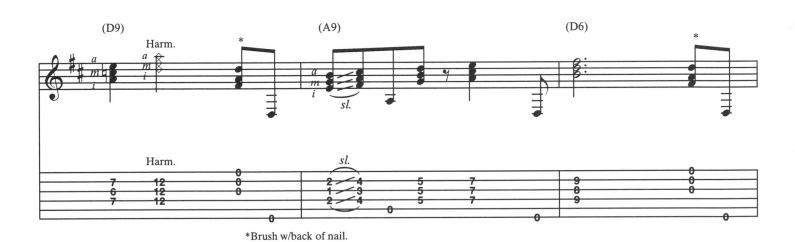

*Brush w/back of nail.

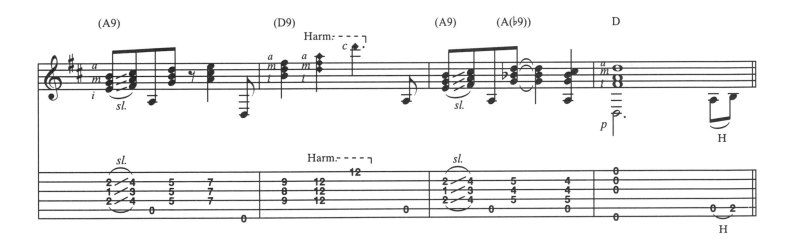

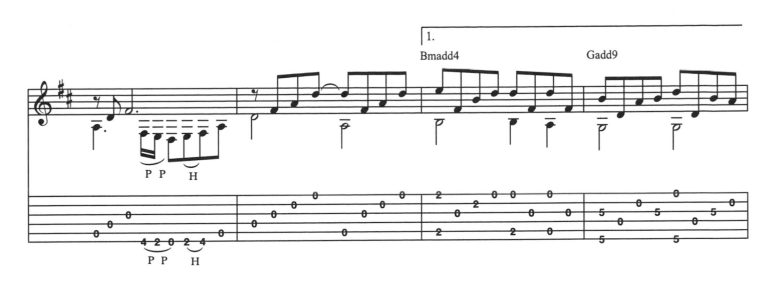

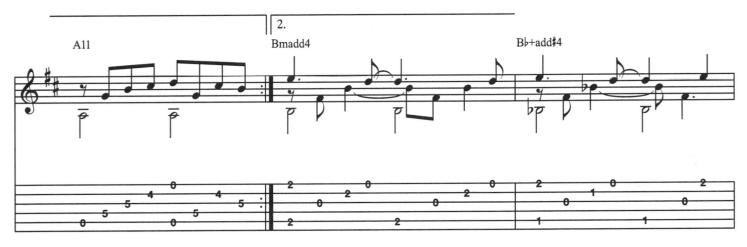

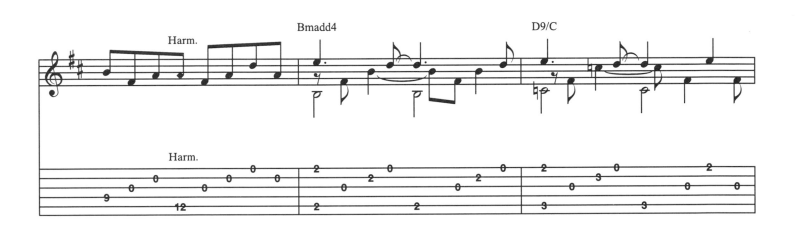

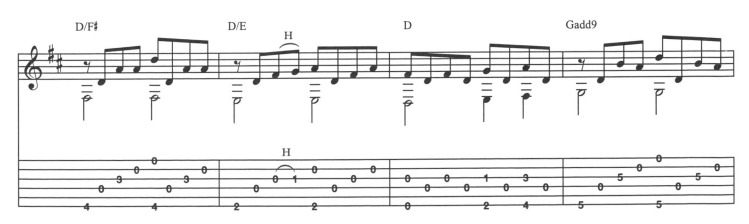

44

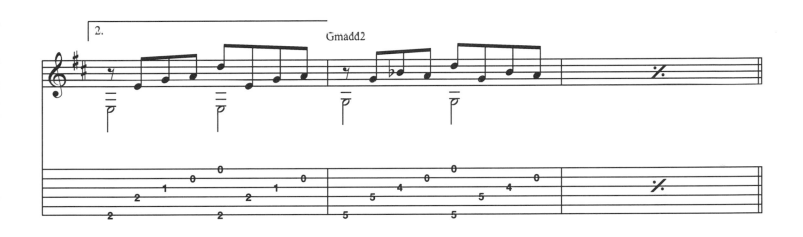

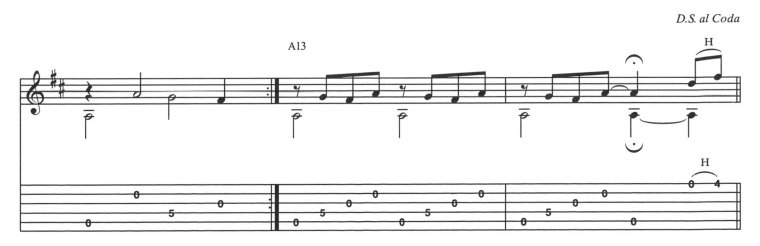

45

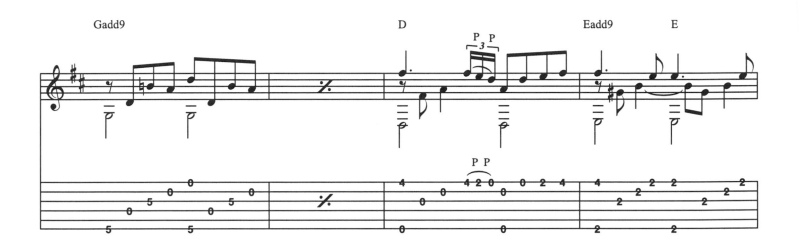

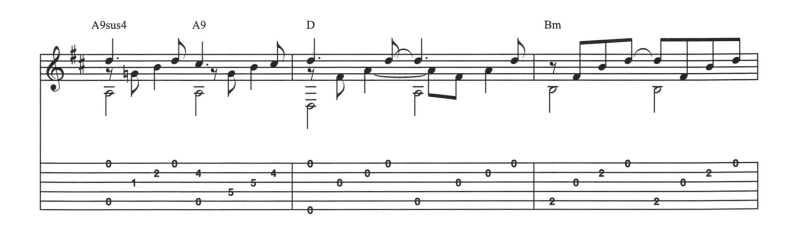

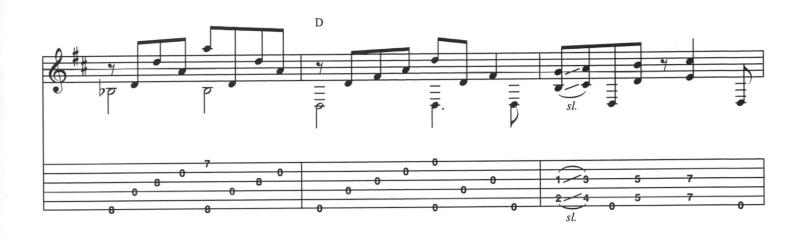

*Brush w/back of nail.

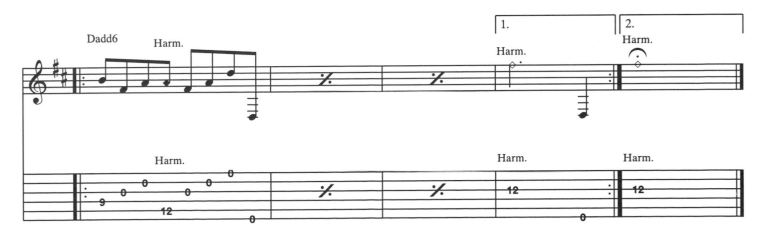

L'AMOUR MANQUÉ

Recorded on Waiting for a Dancer

Music by Adrian Legg

Tuning:
⑥=C ③=G
⑤=G ②=B
④=D ①=E

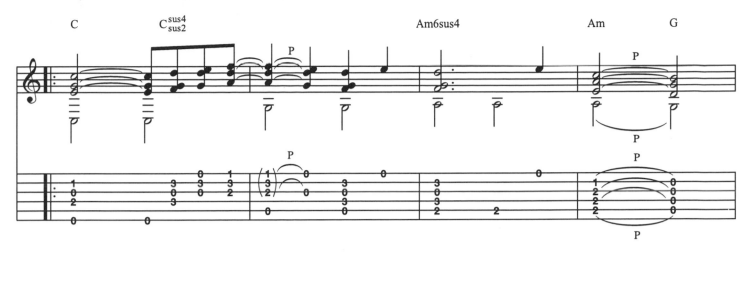

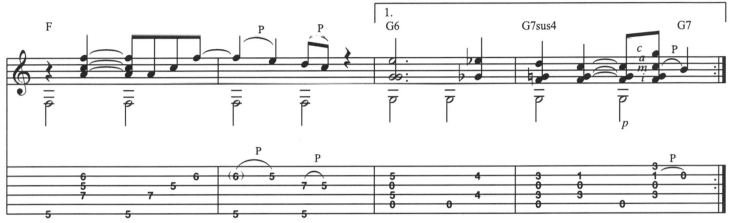

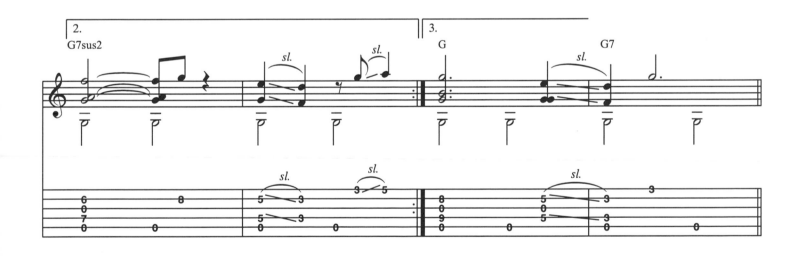

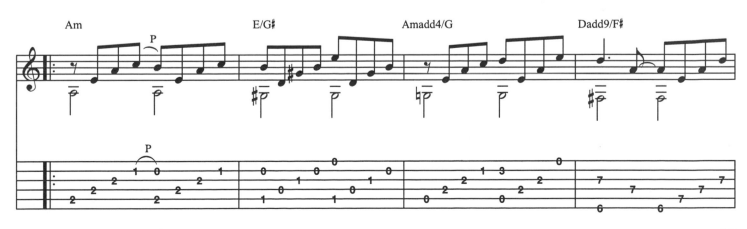

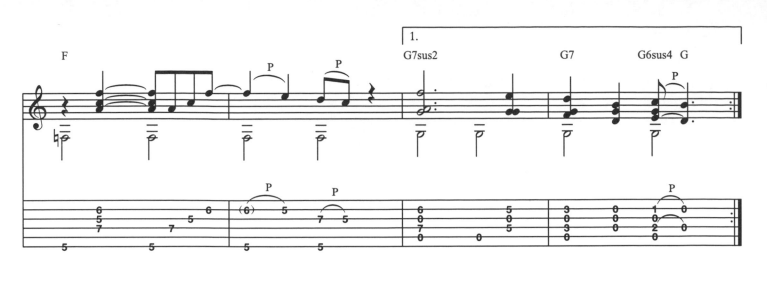

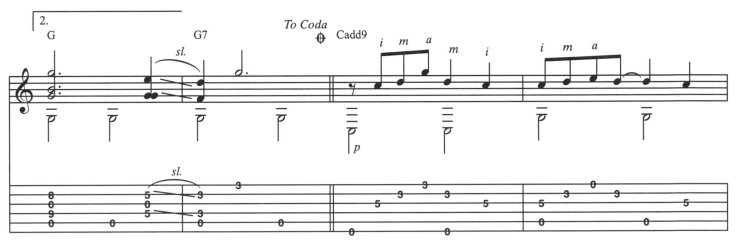

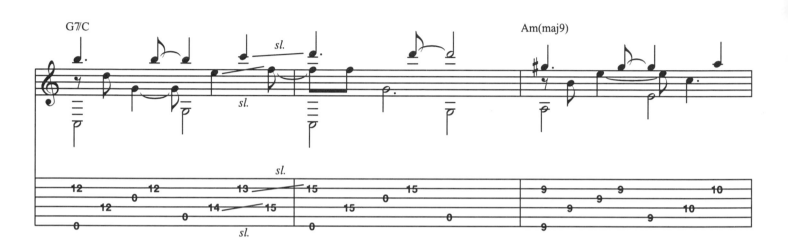

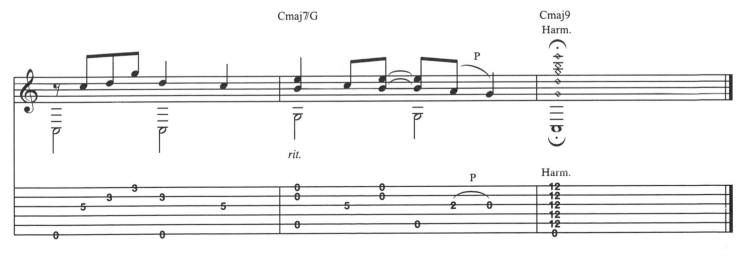

MRS. JACK'S LAST STAND
Recorded on Guitar for Mortals

Music by Adrian Legg

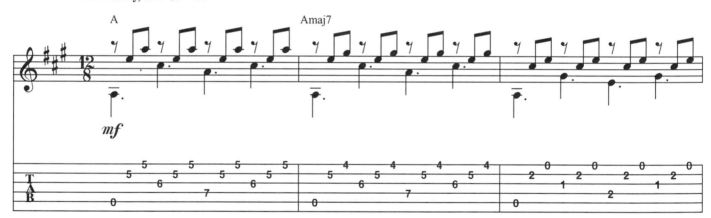

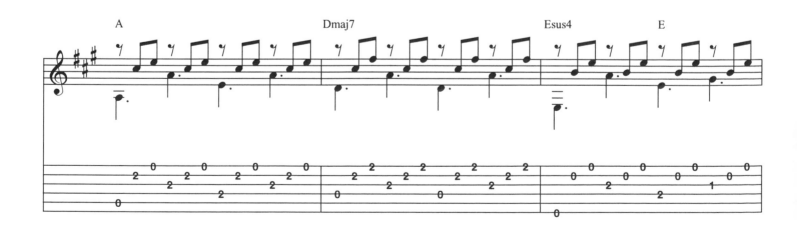

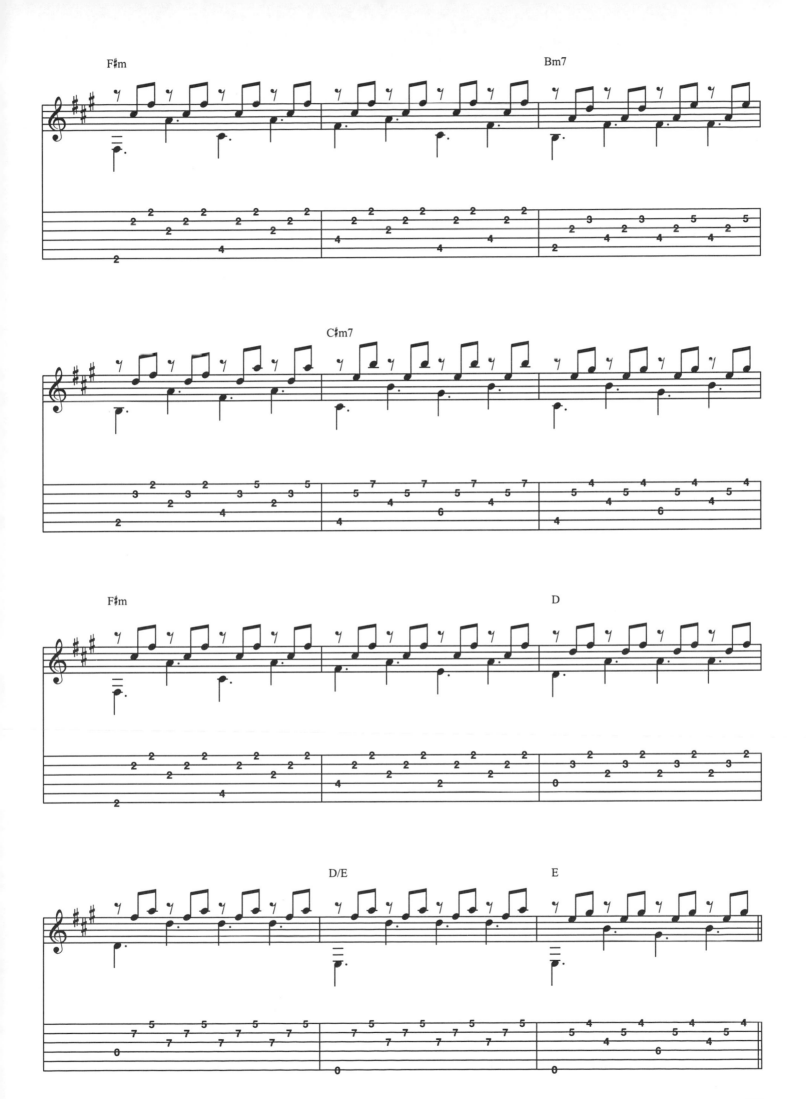

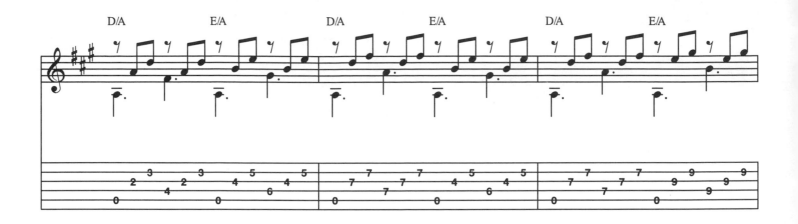

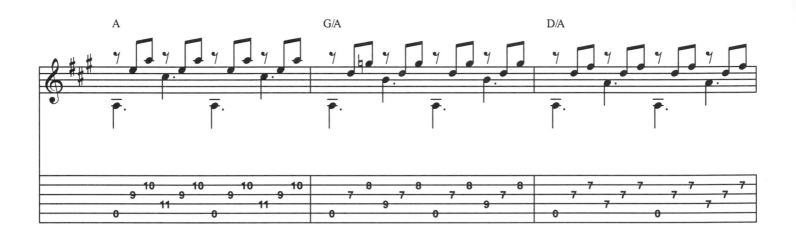

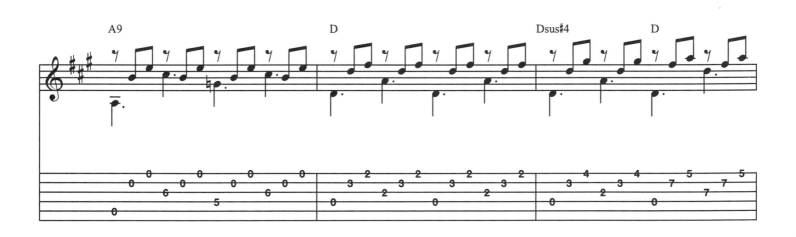

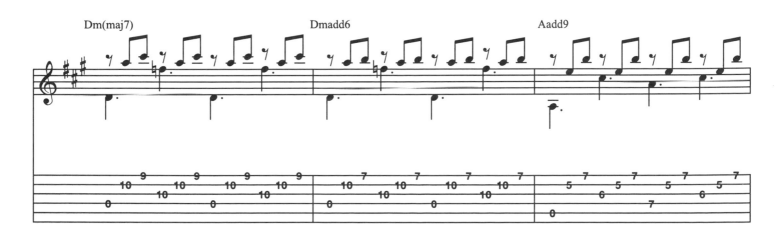

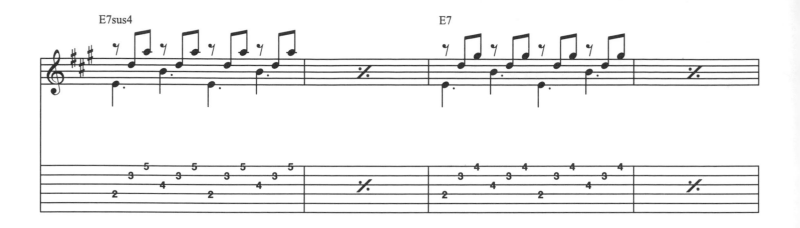

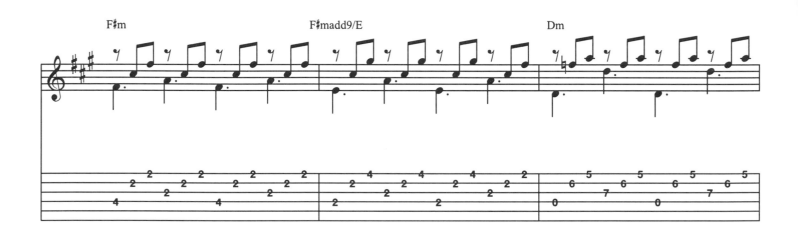

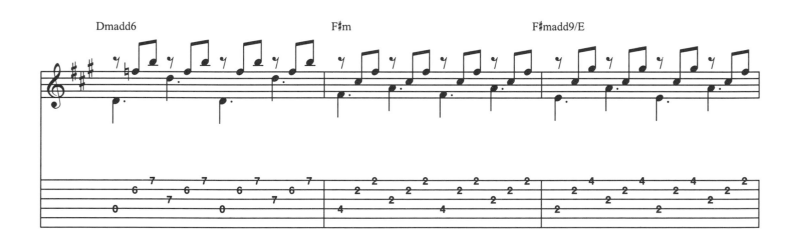

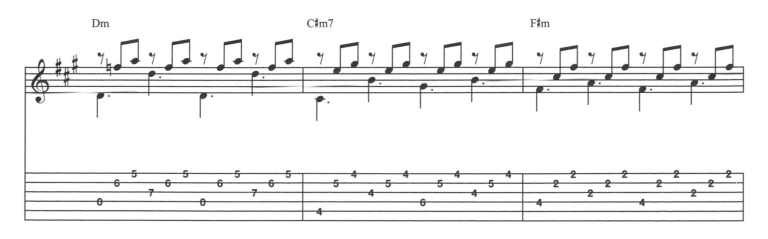

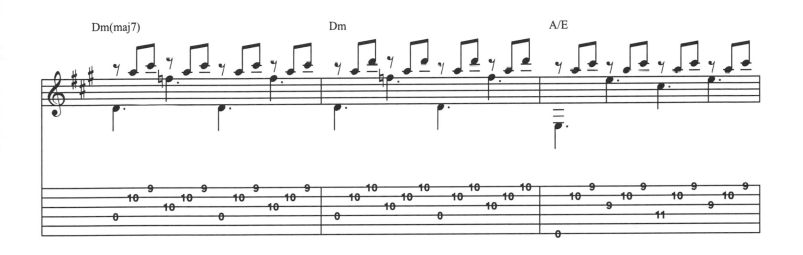

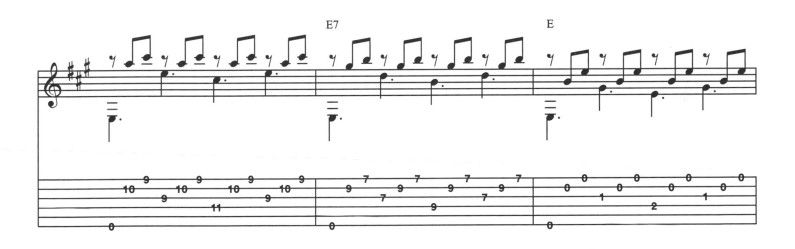

D.C. al Coda

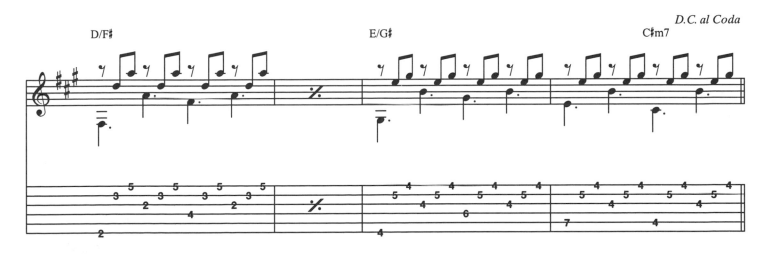

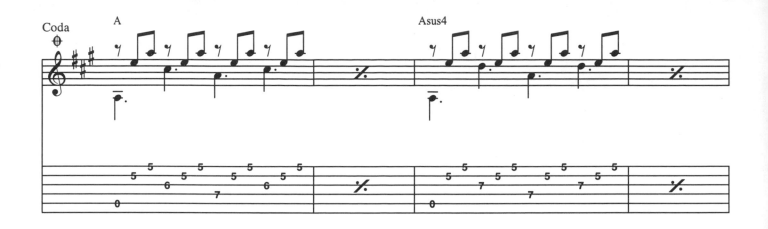

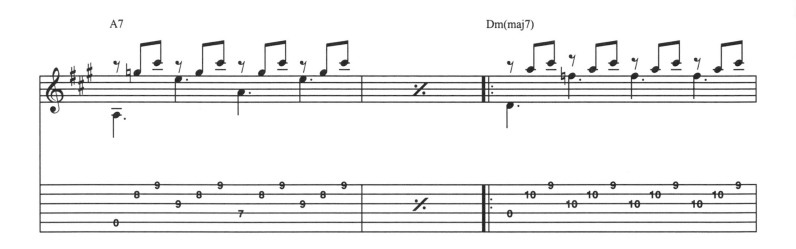

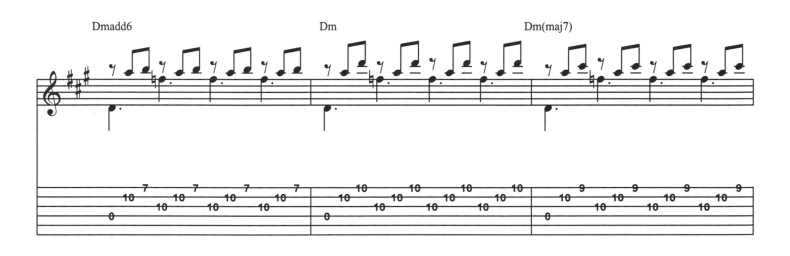

NANCI

Recorded on Guitar for Mortals

Music by Adrian Legg

Tuning:
⑥=D ③=G
⑤=G ②=B
④=D ①=E

Moderately, in 2 ♩ = 116

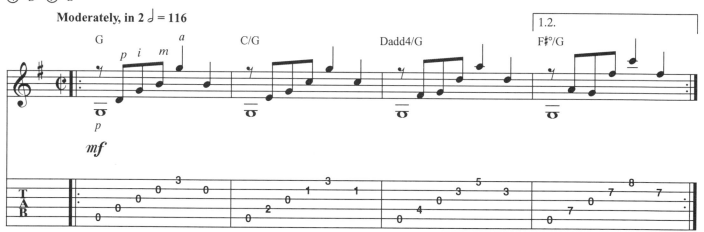

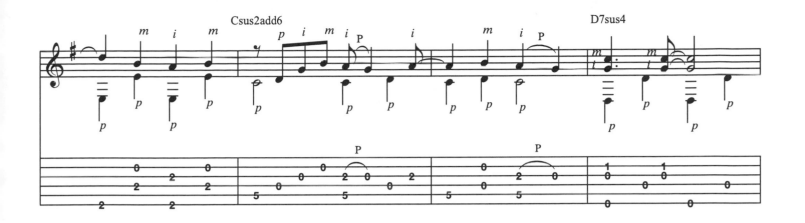

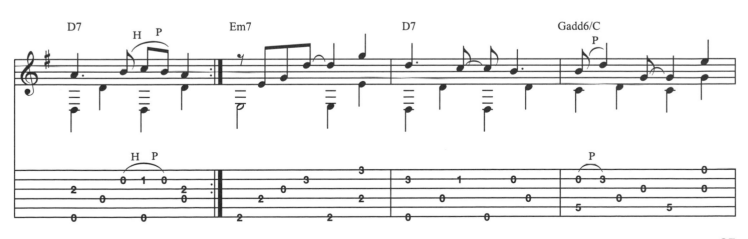

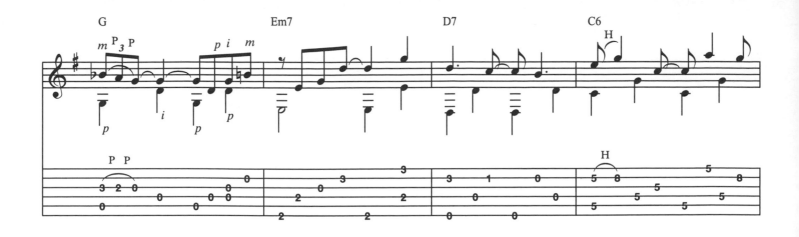

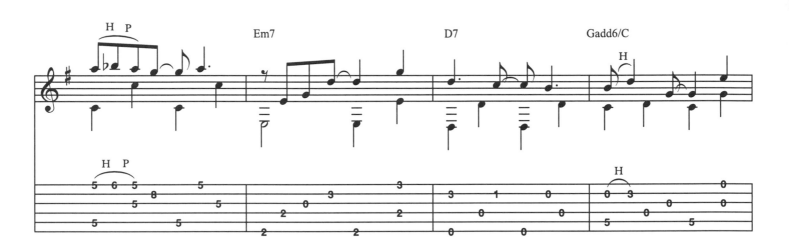

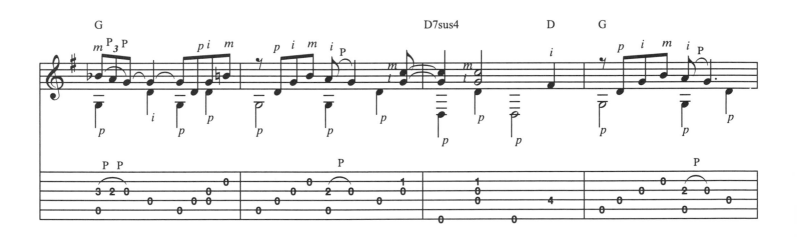

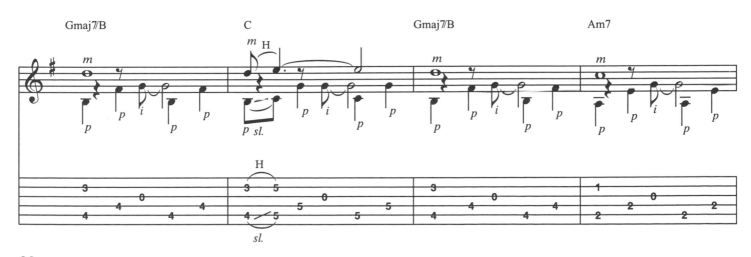

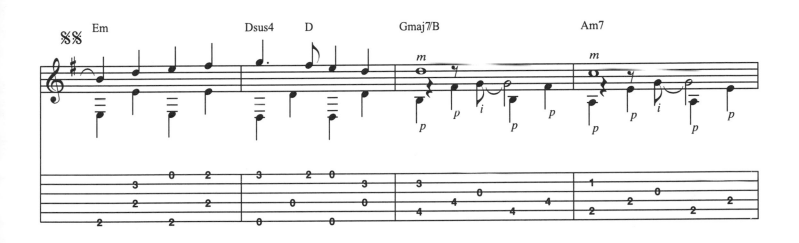

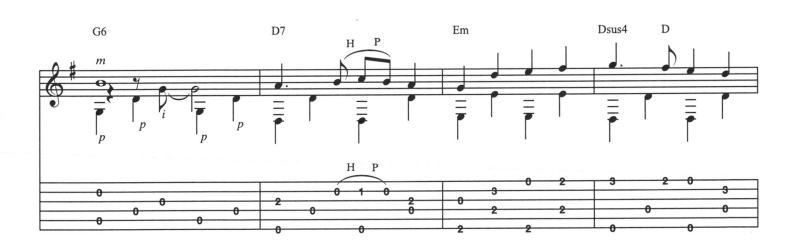

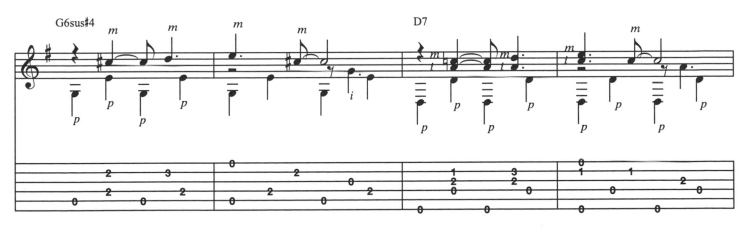

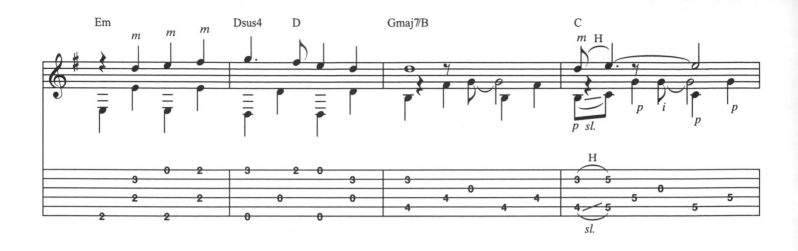

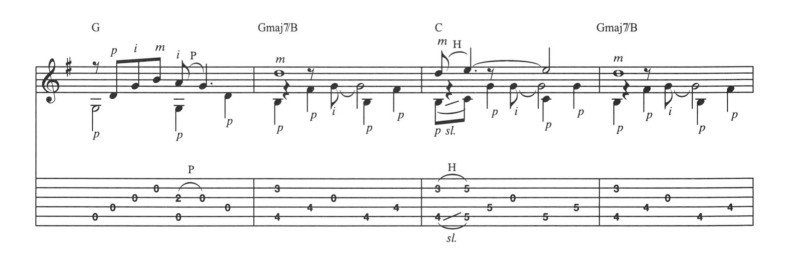

2nd time to Coda I;
3rd time to Coda II

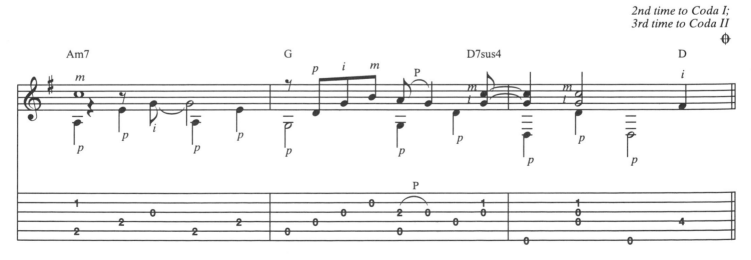

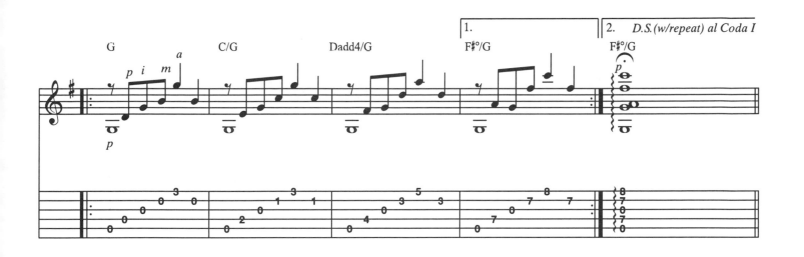

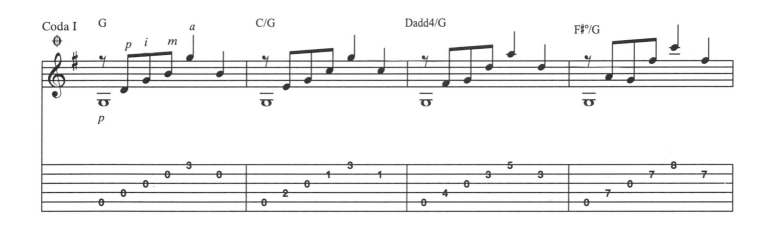

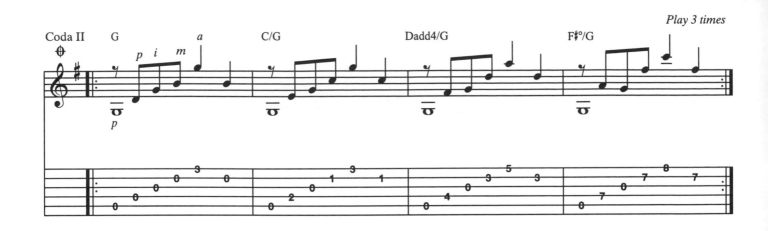

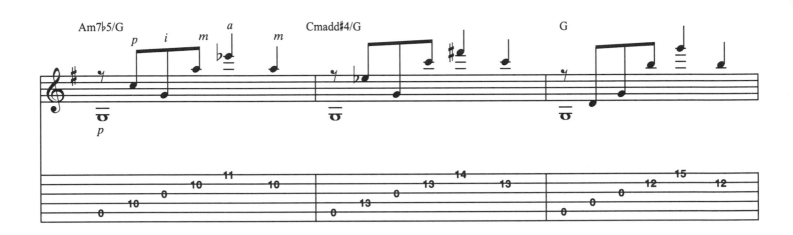

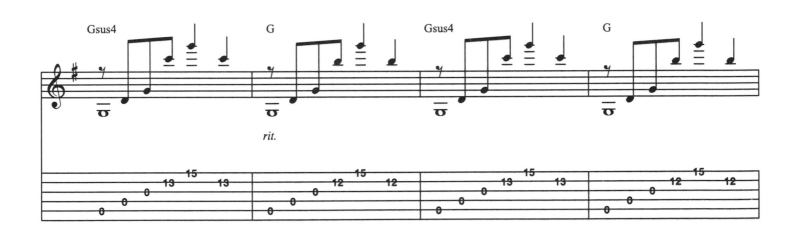

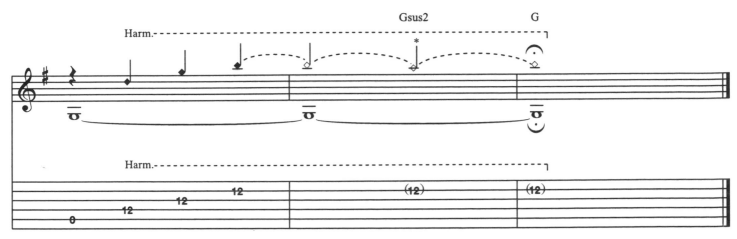

*Tune 2nd string down a whole step to A, then back up to B.

MRS. CROWE'S BLUE WALTZ

Recorded on Mrs. Crowe's Blue Waltz

Music by Adrian Legg

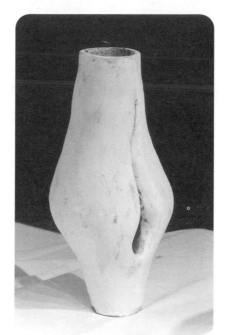

Tuning:
⑥=C ③=G
⑤=G ②=B
④=D ①=E

Freely

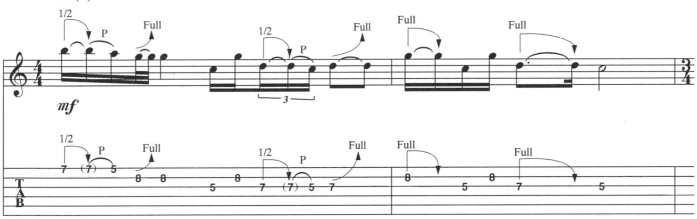

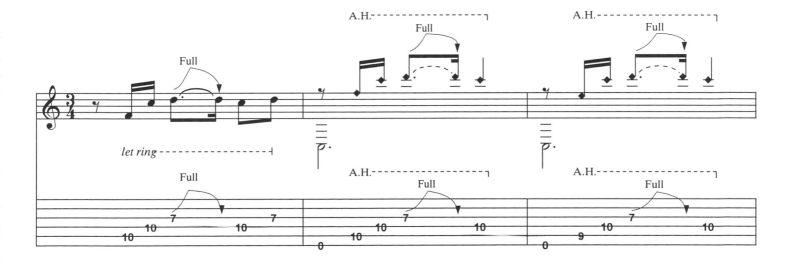

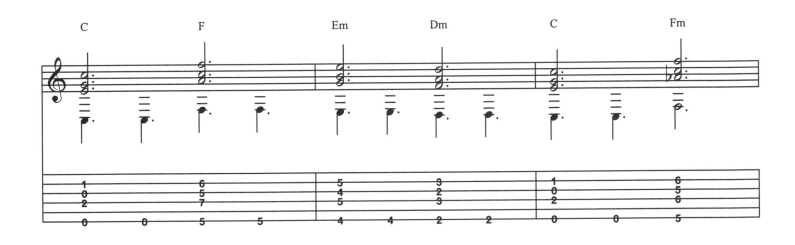

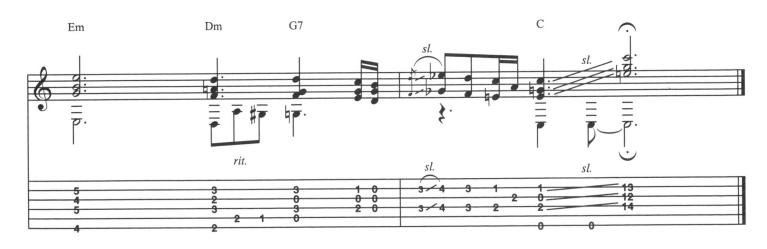

CHICKEN LICKEN'S LAST RIDE

Recorded on Guitar for Mortals

Music by Adrian Legg

Tuning:
⑥=D ③=G
⑤=G ②=B
④=D ①=E

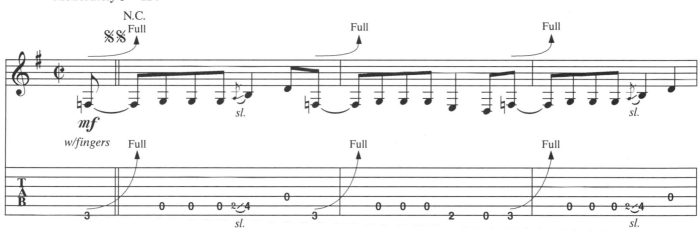

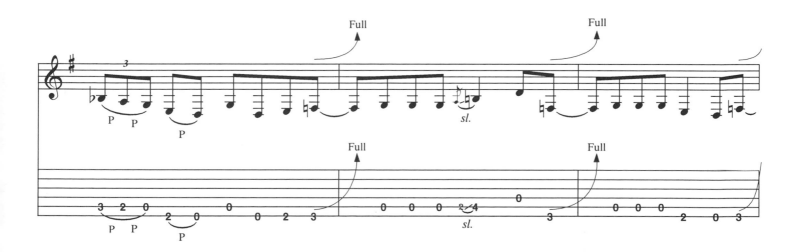

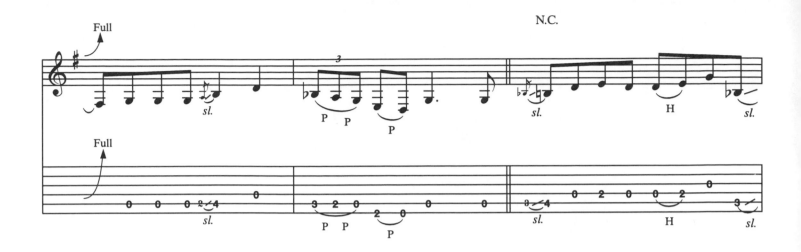

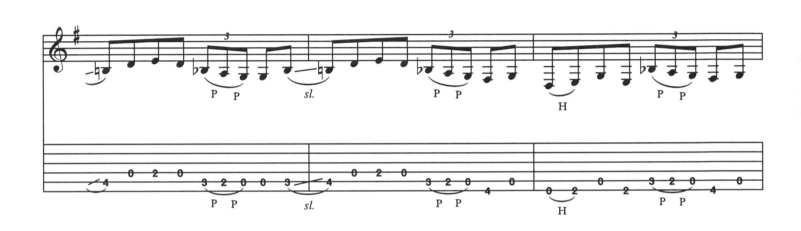

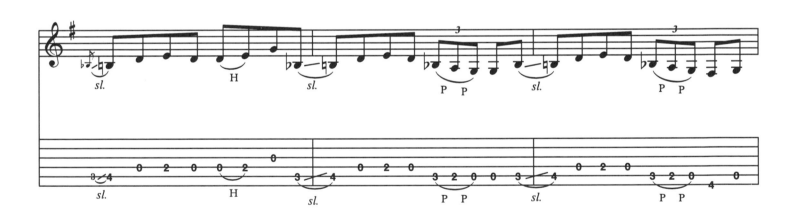

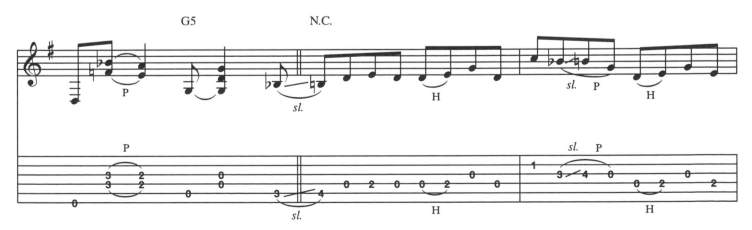

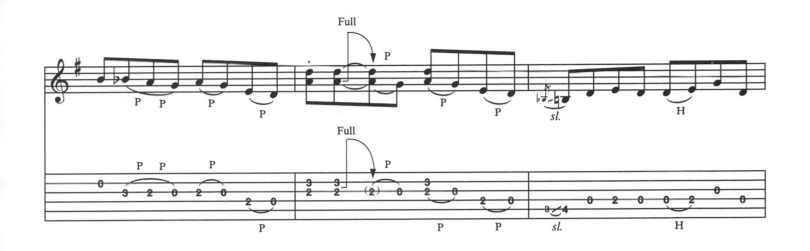

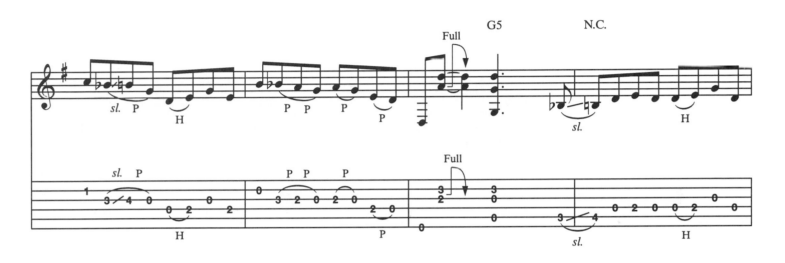

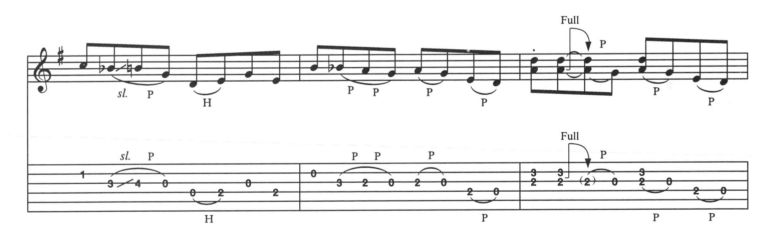

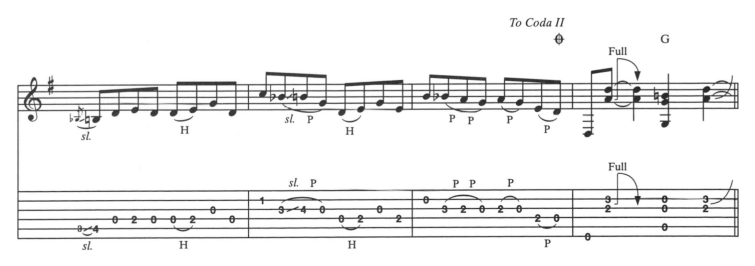

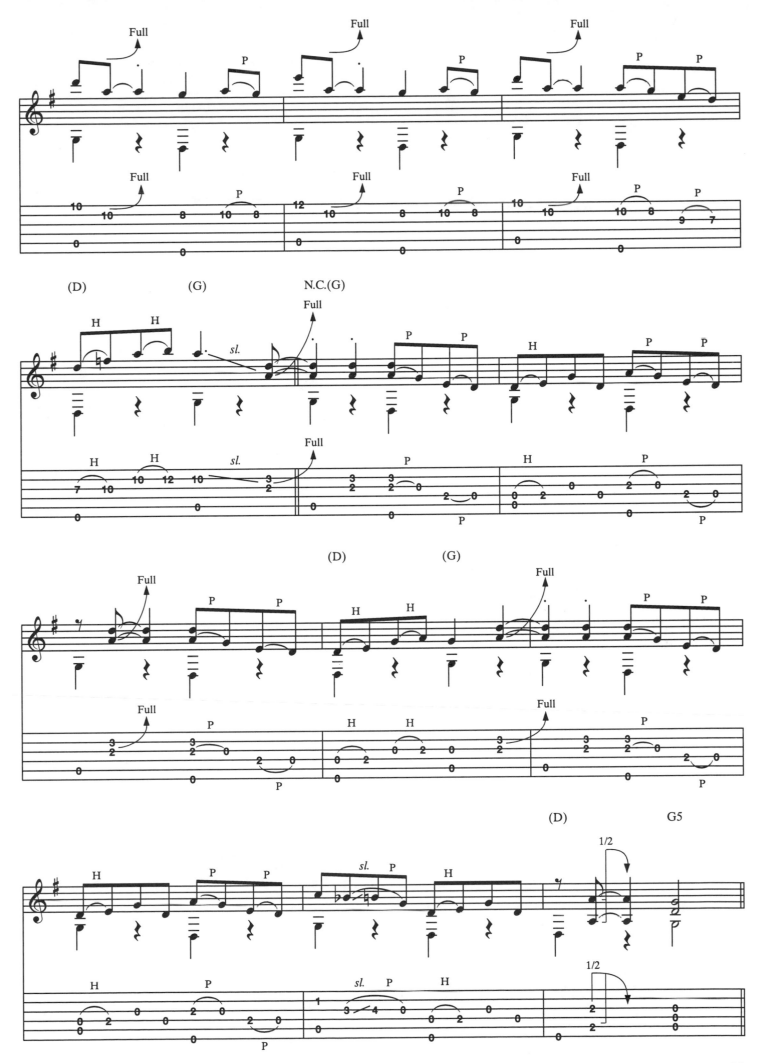

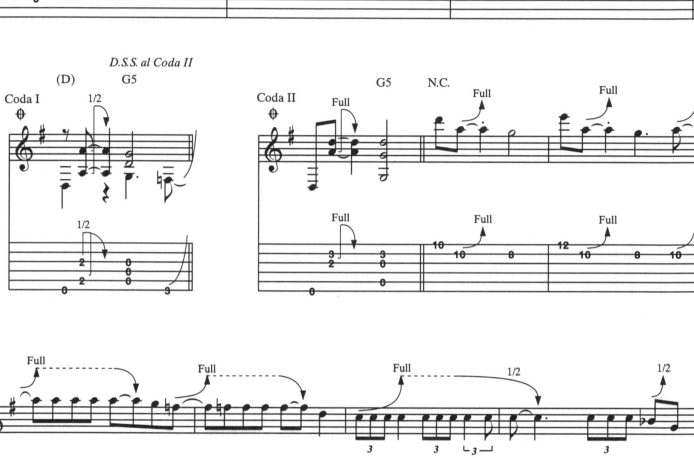

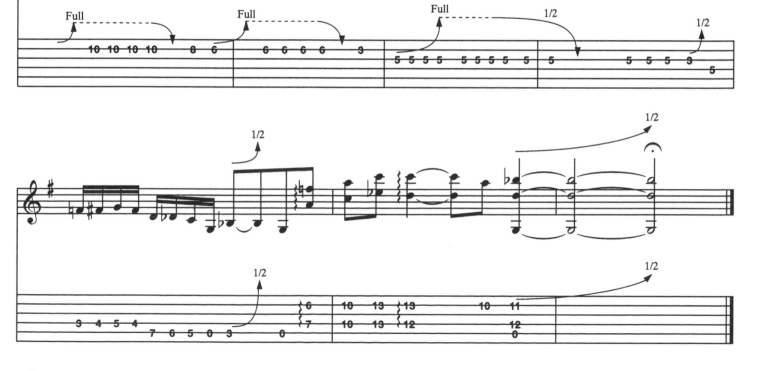